W9-AWO-456

al forno

al forno

oven-baked dishes from Italy

maxine clark photography by peter cassidy

RYLAND
PETERS
& SMALL

LONDON NEW YORK

First published in the USA in 2003
Ryland Peters & Small, Inc.
519 Broadway, 5th Floor
New York, NY 10012
www.rylandpeters.com

10 9 8 7 6 5 4 3 2 1

Library of Congress Cataloging-in-Publication Data

Clark, Maxine.

  Al forno : oven-baked dishes from italy / Maxine Clark ;
photography by Peter Cassidy.

    p. cm.

  ISBN 1-84172-500-5

  1. Baking–Italy. 2. Cookery, Italian. I. Title.

  TX765.C54 2003

  641.8'15'0945–dc21

                            2003000670

Printed in China

Designer Luana Gobbo
Commissioning Editor Elsa Petersen-Schepelern
Editor Susan Stuck
Production Meryl Silbert
Art Director Gabriella Le Grazie
Publishing Director Alison Starling

Food Stylist Maxine Clark
Assistant Food Stylists Lizzie Harris, Kate
Habershon, and Laura Lennox-Conyngham
Props Stylist Antonia Gaunt

Notes

All spoon measurements are level unless otherwise
indicated.

All eggs are large unless otherwise specified.
Uncooked or partially cooked eggs should not
be served to the very young, the very old, those
with compromised immune systems, or to
pregnant women.

contents

6   *al forno ...*

8   vegetables

32 fish and seafood

44 meat and poultry

56 sweet things

64 index

al forno is where the heart is …

The Italian words *al forno* mean "in the oven," and so when something is described as *Cannelloni al Forno* on a menu, it means that it has been cooked in the oven. *Al forno* can also mean roasted or braised, in fact anything that has passed through a hot oven.

Ever since I was little, these words conjured up in my mind a magical place in Italy—a country kitchen where the iron stove was the center of family life. The wood-fired oven would always be on and enticing smells would permeate the whole house, leading people by their noses into the kitchen. The secrets within would be revealed when the black door swung open and the contents were carefully lifted out onto a massive scrubbed wooden table for all to admire.

The versatility of the oven is quite amazing. It can cope with delicate buttery pastries, a rustic loaf, an aromatic stew, a braised fish, or a roasted bird—the smell of each being very individual and whetting the appetite before we even see the dish. The oven will brown and caramelize roasted meat if cooked uncovered at a high temperature. Turn the temperature down and cook something in a closed baking dish and the contents will simmer and braise in their own juices to produce an aromatic and tender dish. The heat inside can be dry and fast to give a golden crust on a creamy pasta dish or loaf of bread. We can leave a stew to simmer all day, forgetting about it, but remembering as soon as the scent starts to waft through the oven door.

Al forno is definitely where the heart is.

vegetables

These firm but juicy tomatoes burst with the flavor of the sun. They take no time to prepare, but need a long time in the oven and smell fantastic while cooking. Plum tomatoes have less moisture and work well, but you can use any vine-ripened variety, just as long as they have some taste.

slow-roasted tomatoes with garlic and oregano
pomodori al forno

Cut the tomatoes in half lengthwise (around the middle if using round tomatoes). Put them cut side up on the baking sheet.

Put the garlic, oregano, olive oil, salt, and pepper in a bowl and mix well, then spoon or brush the mixture over the cut tomatoes.

Bake in a preheated oven at 325°F for 1½–2 hours, checking every now and then. The tomatoes should be slightly shrunk but still brilliantly red after cooking (if they are too dark, they will taste bitter).

Serve topped with basil leaves as an accompaniment to grills and fish, or use on top of bruschetta.

6–10 ripe plum tomatoes

2 garlic cloves, finely chopped

1 tablespoon dried oregano

¼ cup extra virgin olive oil

sea salt and freshly ground black pepper

basil leaves, to serve

a baking sheet

serves 4

In Sicily, onions are roasted in huge metal trays, then put on display outside vegetable stores. Sicilians love the sweetness of onions cooked like this. Normally the onions are simply squeezed out of their skins after roasting. However, I think they taste even better finished off with a sweet and sour sauce.

whole onions baked in their skins
cipolle arrostite al forno

Trim the root end of each onion so that they will stand up securely. Rub with olive oil. Cut a deep cross in the top of each one, slicing towards the base so that it is cut almost into quarters.

Pack closely together in a flameproof roasting pan. Sprinkle with oil, salt, and pepper. Bake in a preheated oven at 375°F for about 45 minutes to 1 hour, until tender in the center.

Lift out the onions onto a serving dish, leaving the juices behind. Set the roasting pan over medium heat and add the wine, vinegar, raisins, fennel seeds, and capers. Scrape up any sediment and boil for a couple of minutes until reduced and syrupy.

Taste, add salt and pepper if necessary, then pour the sauce over the onions and sprinkle with chopped parsley.

6 large white, red, or yellow onions

olive oil, for basting and serving

⅔ cup white wine

3 tablespoons red wine vinegar

2 tablespoons golden raisins

1 teaspoon fennel seeds

1 tablespoon small salted capers, rinsed

sea salt and freshly ground black pepper

2–3 tablespoons chopped fresh flat-leaf parsley, to serve

a flameproof roasting pan

serves 6

zucchini and tomatoes baked with fontina

zucchine ripiene con pomodori e fontina

Zucchini are much more flavorful when cooked this way—bathed in garlic and olive oil, then stuffed with sweet, ripe cherry tomatoes and enveloped in melting fontina cheese. Delightfully fresh and summery.

Halve the zucchini lengthwise and trim a little off the uncut sides so that they will sit still like boats. Using a teaspoon, scoop out the soft-seeded centers. Arrange the boats in a row in the prepared dish.

Put the garlic, olive oil, salt, and pepper in a bowl, stir well, then brush over the cut surfaces of the zucchini. Arrange the halved tomatoes in the grooves. Season well, then sprinkle with olive oil and bread crumbs. Bake in a preheated oven at 325°F for 30 minutes.

Remove from the oven and arrange the cheese over the zucchini and tomatoes. Return the dish to the oven for another 10 minutes to melt the cheese. Serve immediately while the cheese is still bubbling.

6 medium zucchini (as straight as possible)

2 garlic cloves, chopped

2 tablespoons olive oil, plus extra for sprinkling

about 30 cherry tomatoes, halved

3–4 tablespoons dry bread crumbs

8 oz. fontina cheese, sliced

sea salt and freshly ground black pepper

a shallow ovenproof dish, greased

serves 6

eggplant, tomato, and parmesan gratin
melanzane, pomodori e parmigiano al forno

A pretty gratin bursting with flavor. Tomato halves are baked with briefly fried, thinly sliced eggplant and freshly grated Parmesan.

Cut the eggplant lengthwise into ¼-inch slices. Sprinkle with salt and let drain in a colander for 30 minutes. Rinse well and pat dry with paper towels. Cut the tomatoes in half through the middle.

Heat the oil in a skillet and sauté the eggplant in batches until deep golden brown. Drain on paper towels. Arrange a layer of eggplant in the prepared dish, then top with a layer of tomato halves, cut side up. Sprinkle with the chopped basil, salt, pepper, and half of the Parmesan. Add another layer of eggplant, then the remaining Parmesan.

Bake the gratin in a preheated oven at 400°F for 25–30 minutes, or until browned and bubbling on top. Let cool slightly and serve warm, or cool completely and serve as a salad.

1 large eggplant

1 lb. very ripe, red tomatoes

about ⅔ cup olive oil

¼ cup chopped fresh basil

1¼ cups freshly grated Parmesan cheese

sea salt and freshly ground black pepper

a shallow ovenproof dish, well buttered

serves 4

potato and mushroom gratin

tortiera di patate e funghi al forno

Baking sliced potatoes and mushrooms in layers lets the potatoes absorb the juices and earthy flavor of the mushrooms. Try to use the darkest mushrooms you can find—they will have the best taste. You can always mix fresh ones with reconstituted dried mushrooms for a more intense flavor.

Peel the potatoes and slice thickly, putting them in a bowl of cold water as you go. Trim the mushrooms and slice thickly. Put half the potatoes in a layer in the bottom of the dish, sprinkle with olive oil, and cover with half the mushrooms.

Put the bread crumbs, Parmesan, parsley, salt, and pepper in a bowl and mix well. Spread half this mixture over the mushrooms, then sprinkle with more olive oil. Cover with a layer of potatoes, sprinkle with olive oil, then add a layer of the remaining mushrooms. Finally, sprinkle with the remaining bread crumb mixture and more oil.

Cover with foil and bake in a preheated oven at 350°F for 30 minutes. Uncover and cook for a further 30 minutes until the potatoes are tender and the top is golden brown.

Note If you blanch the potato slices first for 5 minutes in boiling salted water, they will take only 30 minutes to cook.

2 lb. medium potatoes

1½ lb. flavorsome mushrooms such as portobello (or use fresh wild mushrooms)

extra virgin olive oil, for sprinkling

3½ cups stale (not dry) white bread crumbs

¼ cup freshly grated Parmesan cheese

¼ cup chopped fresh flat-leaf parsley

sea salt and freshly ground black pepper

a deep gratin or other ovenproof dish, well buttered

serves 4

beans simmered in a chianti flask

fagioli nel fiasco

Beans were traditionally cooked this way in Tuscany when Chianti flasks were plentiful and blown from one piece of glass. The flask was embedded in the glowing ashes of the hearth to cook for as long as possible. You can use a casserole dish in the oven—it's just not as romantic. The beans emerge deliciously creamy and need only a few drops of olive oil. Toscanelli beans are traditionally used because they are small and won't stick in the neck of the flask when cooked, but they are hard to find.

2½ cups small dried white beans

2 garlic cloves, unpeeled

6–8 sage leaves

¾ cup extra virgin olive oil, plus extra for sprinkling

sea salt and freshly ground black pepper

an ovenproof casserole dish or beanpot, or a hand-blown Chianti flask and a roasting pan

a circle of waxed paper (see method), plus extra waxed paper or cheesecloth

serves 4

Put the beans into an ovenproof casserole, beanpot, or hand-blown Chianti flask—don't use a modern molded flask with a seam, because it may crack. Add the whole unpeeled garlic cloves, sage, olive oil, salt, and pepper. Pour in enough warm water to fill the flask three-quarters full—or, if using a casserole dish or beanpot, pour in 3 times the volume of the other ingredients.

Plug the neck of the flask with scrunched up waxed paper or rolled and folded cheesecloth—this allows the contents to "breathe" and stops the flask exploding. If using a casserole or beanpot, make sure it has a tight-fitting lid.

Put the flask on its side in a roasting pan half-filled with hot water and cook in the oven 325°F at for 3 hours, turning every now and then. If using a casserole dish or beanpot, cover with a lid and put it in the oven the same temperature and cook for 2 hours, then put a circle of waxed paper directly on top of the beans to keep in the moisture. Cover and return to the oven for another hour. The beans must be very tender and absorb most of the water and oil.

When cooked, transfer the beans to a heated serving dish and dress liberally with olive oil, then taste and season with salt and pepper. This dish is best served hot, with Italian sausages or roast pork, or as a simple appetizer with bread.

spinach and ricotta timbales with sun-dried tomatoes, olives, capers, and herbs

timballi di ricotta, spinaci e condimenti

These are like little savory cheesecakes, served warm with a sprinkle of olive oil or a small spoonful of rich tomato sauce. I always strain the ricotta for this dish, because it makes the mixture lighter. Beat the eggs into the cheese very well for even more lightness, and be careful with the seasoning—the capers and olives are quite salty already.

Put a sun-dried tomato in the bottom of each mold or ramekin. Thinly slice the remaining sun-dried tomatoes.

To prepare the spinach, remove the tough stems from the leaves, then wash the leaves well and put in a saucepan while still wet. Cook until the leaves wilt, then plunge into cold water. Drain very well and squeeze to extract any excess moisture. Loosen the leaves slightly.

Push the ricotta through a fine-mesh sieve or food mill to make it fluffy, then beat in the eggs. Lightly stir in the drained, wilted spinach, sliced sun-dried tomatoes, olives, basil or oregano, and capers. Taste and season with salt, pepper, and nutmeg. Spoon the ricotta mixture into the molds and level, then put on the baking sheet.

Bake in a preheated oven at 375°F for 20 minutes until almost set and a little puffed. Remove from the oven and let cool slightly. Invert the molds onto small plates, then serve at room temperature with extra capers and a sprinkle of olive oil or a spoonful of fresh tomato sauce.

10 sun-dried (or sun-blushed) tomatoes in oil, drained

8 oz. fresh leaf spinach, about 3 cups torn

1 lb. ricotta cheese, well drained, about 2 cups

3 large eggs, beaten

12 oven-dried black olives, such as Kalamata, pitted and coarsely chopped

2 tablespoons chopped fresh basil or oregano

2 tablespoons salted capers, rinsed and chopped, plus extra whole capers to serve

freshly grated nutmeg

olive oil or fresh tomato sauce, for sprinkling

sea salt and freshly ground black pepper

6 dariole molds or ½-cup ramekins, generously buttered

a baking sheet

serves 6

three-colored rice and cheese cake

torta di riso e formaggio tricolore

Ideal for an indulgent lunch or supper dish, this creamy rice cake oozes with mozzarella, and has pockets of tomatoes bursting with flavor. You could even add a layer of cubed mozzarella to the middle of the tart, so that the center exudes strings of melted cheese when you cut it.

Dust the prepared cake pan with the cornmeal or dried bread crumbs.

If using fresh spinach, tear off the stems. Wash the leaves well, then put them, still wet, in a covered saucepan and cook for a few minutes until wilted. Drain well but do not squeeze dry—you want large pieces of spinach. If using thawed spinach, lightly squeeze it to remove excess moisture and toss the leaves a little to loosen them. Mix the spinach into the beaten eggs.

Cook the rice in a large saucepan of boiling salted water for 10 minutes, until almost tender, then drain through a strainer. Meanwhile, heat the oil and butter in a skillet. Add the onion and cook until golden. Stir into the rice.

Season the egg and spinach mixture with nutmeg, salt, and pepper. Stir into the rice, then fold in the cherry tomatoes, cubed mozzarella, and Parmesan. Spoon into the prepared cake pan and level the surface.

Bake in a preheated oven at 400°F for about 25–30 minutes, until firm and golden. Invert onto a plate, cut into wedges, and serve hot.

¼ cup cornmeal or dried bread crumbs

about 4 cups fresh or 8 oz. frozen whole leaf spinach, thawed

3 eggs, beaten

2 cups plus 2 tablespoons Italian arborio risotto rice (not long-grain)

1 tablespoon olive oil

2 tablespoons butter

1 onion, finely chopped

freshly grated nutmeg

8 oz. tiny cherry tomatoes

6 oz. mozzarella cheese, drained and cubed

¼ cup freshly grated Parmesan cheese

sea salt and freshly ground black pepper

a nonstick springform cake pan, 8-inches diameter, well buttered

serves 6

fresh egg pasta

Homemade pasta is a delight and it's not hard to do. The quantities given are only guidelines—you may need more flour depending on the humidity and type of flour used. But don't add too much or the pasta will be tough.

1⅓ cups Italian-style flour or all-purpose*

a pinch of salt

2 eggs

1 tablespoon olive oil

semolina flour, for dusting

a pasta machine

a piece of dowelling

serves 2–4

*I like to use use half all-purpose flour and half fine semolina flour to give more bite to the pasta. You can also use all fine semolina flour, which is harder to work but has a wonderful texture.

Sift the flour and salt onto a clean work surface and make a well in the center. Beat the eggs and oil together and pour into the well. Gradually mix the eggs into the flour with the fingers of one hand, bringing it together to form a dough.

Knead the dough until smooth, then wrap in plastic, and let rest for at least 30 minutes before attempting to roll it out. The pasta will be much more elastic after resting.

Feed the rested dough several times through the widest setting on the pasta machine, folding in three each time. Then continue to pass it through the machine, reducing the settings until you reach the required thickness. Generally, the second from last setting is best for tagliatelle and lasagne—the finest is for ravioli or other filled pasta.

When you reach the required thickness, hang the pasta over the length of dowelling to dry a little—this will make it easier to cut because it won't be too sticky. Pass it through the chosen cutters, then transfer to a tray covered with a clean dish towel and sprinkled with a little semolina flour. Toss the pasta lightly in the flour and use straight away. Alternatively, drape over the dowelling again until ready to cook.

Variation

Spinach pasta Sift the flour onto a clean work surface and make a well in the center. Cook 6 oz. package frozen leaf spinach until wilted, then squeeze out the moisture. Mix with a pinch of salt, 1 whole egg, and 1 yolk. Pour into the well in the flour and continue as for the basic recipe.

green lasagne with ricotta pesto and mushrooms

lasagne verdi

To make the mushroom sauce, drain the soaked mushrooms, reserving the soaking liquid. Squeeze them gently, then chop coarsely. Heat half the oil and all the butter in a large skillet. When foaming, add half the fresh and chopped dried mushrooms and half the onion. Sauté over high heat for 4–5 minutes until tender. Repeat with the remaining mushrooms and onions, then mix the 2 batches in the pan. Stir in the garlic and herbs and cook for 2 minutes. Add the stock and soaking liquid, then boil for 4–5 minutes until the sauce is syrupy. Let cool.

To make the pesto, pound the garlic, pine nuts, and salt with a mortar and pestle. Add the basil leaves, a few at a time, pounding to a paste. Gradually beat in the olive oil until creamy. Beat in the butter, season with pepper, then beat in the Parmesan. Alternatively, put everything in a food processor and blend until smooth. Transfer to a bowl, add the ricotta, and stir well.

Bring a large saucepan of salted water to a boil and drop in a few lasagne sheets at a time. Fresh pasta is cooked when the water returns to a boil. Lift it out and drain over the sides of a colander. If using dried lasagne, follow the instructions on the package.

Line the prepared dish with a layer of lasagne and add a layer of ricotta pesto. Add another layer of pasta, a layer of mushroom sauce, then a layer of lasagne. Repeat until all the ingredients have been used, finishing with a layer of lasagne. Sprinkle with Parmesan and dot with butter.

Cover with oiled aluminum foil and bake in a preheated oven at 350°F for 20 minutes. Uncover, then bake for a further 20 minutes until golden. Let stand for 10 minutes before serving.

8 oz. fresh spinach lasagne (see page 24), or 1 package dried green lasagne

mushroom sauce

1 oz. dried porcini mushrooms, soaked in warm water for 20 minutes

¼ cup olive oil

4 tablespoons unsalted butter

2 lb. fresh wild mushrooms or portobellos, thinly sliced

1 onion, chopped

4 garlic cloves, chopped

¼ cup chopped fresh flat-leaf parsley

2–3 sprigs of thyme, chopped

1¼ cups chicken or vegetable stock

ricotta pesto

3 garlic cloves

1 cup pine nuts, 3 oz.

3½ cups fresh basil leaves

⅔ cup olive oil

6 tablespoons unsalted butter, softened, plus extra to serve

¼ cup freshly grated Parmesan cheese, plus extra for sprinkling

1 cup fresh ricotta cheese

sea salt and freshly ground black pepper

an ovenproof dish, 12 x 9 x 2 inches, buttered

serves 6

cannelloni with ricotta, bitter greens, and cherry tomato sauce

cannelloni con ricotta, verdure amare e salsa di pomodorini

My version of cannelloni combines a creamy sharp ricotta filling, speckled with slightly bitter green "herbs" (arugula and spinach were classed as herbs in the Middle Ages) and a sweet tomato sauce. The contrast between the sauce and filling is amazing. Italians love their bitter greens and you can find a huge variety on sale in the open-air markets and growing wild in the country.

To make the tomato sauce, heat the oil in a saucepan, add the garlic, and cook until just turning golden. Add the halved tomatoes. They should hiss as they go in—this will slightly caramelize the juices, and concentrate the flavor. Stir well, then simmer for 10 minutes. Stir in the basil and season with salt and pepper (the sauce should still appear quite lumpy). Set aside.

To make the ricotta filling, plunge the salad greens into a saucepan of boiling water for 1 minute, then drain well, squeezing out any excess moisture. Chop finely. Press the ricotta through a fine-mesh sieve into a bowl. Beat in the eggs, then add the chopped greens and half the Parmesan. Season with nutmeg, salt, and pepper. Set aside.

Cook the cannelloni or lasagne sheets in a large saucepan of boiling salted water according to the package instructions. If using homemade pasta, cook for 1 minute. Lift out of the water and drain on a clean dish towel.

Spoon the ricotta filling into a pastry bag fitted with a large round tip. Fill each tube of cannelloni or pipe down the shorter edge of each lasagne sheet and roll it up. Arrange the filled cannelloni tightly together in a single layer in the prepared dish. Spoon over the tomato sauce and sprinkle with the remaining Parmesan.

Bake in a preheated oven at 400°F for 25–30 minutes until bubbling. Serve immediately.

12 dried cannelloni tubes, 12 sheets fresh or dried lasagne or 1 recipe Fresh Egg Pasta (see page 24)

tomato sauce

3 tablespoons olive oil

2 garlic cloves, finely chopped

1½ lb. cherry tomatoes, halved

3 tablespoons chopped fresh basil

sea salt and freshly ground black pepper

ricotta filling

3 oz. bitter salad greens such as arugula, watercress, or spinach, about 1 cup

2 cups ricotta cheese, 16 oz.

2 eggs, beaten

1 cup freshly grated Parmesan cheese

freshly grated nutmeg, to taste

a pastry bag with a large round tip

a shallow ovenproof dish, buttered

serves 4–6

rosemary and onion schiacciata

schiacciata con cipolla e rosmarino

**1 cake compressed yeast,
or 1 package active dry
yeast**

a pinch of sugar

1 cup warm water

2⅓ cups all-purpose flour

2 tablespoons olive oil

¼ teaspoon salt

**1 tablespoon chopped
fresh rosemary**

onion topping

2 lb. onions

**3 tablespoons olive oil,
plus extra for sprinkling**

**1 tablespoon chopped
fresh rosemary**

**6 oz. mozzarella,
thinly sliced**

12 anchovies in oil, drained

**16 black olives, such as
Niçoise, pitted**

**sprigs of rosemary,
to serve**

a large baking sheet, floured

*makes a 12-inch pizza,
serves 4*

Schiacciata is the Tuscan word for flat bread, usually baked on the hearth. It is the ancestor of modern pizza.

To make the pizza dough, beat the fresh yeast and sugar in a small bowl, then beat in the warm water. Leave for 10 minutes until frothy. For other yeasts, use according to the package instructions.

Sift the flour into a large bowl and make a well in the center. Pour in the yeast mixture, olive oil, salt, and rosemary. Mix with a round-bladed knife, then bring the dough together with your hands. Transfer to a floured surface. With clean, dry hands, knead the dough for 10 minutes until smooth, elastic, and quite soft. (If too soft to handle, knead in a little more flour.) Place in a clean oiled bowl, cover with a damp dish towel, and let rise for about 1 hour or until doubled in size.

Finely slice the onions. Heat the oil in a heavy saucepan. Add the onions and cook over gentle heat, stirring occasionally, for 40 minutes to 1 hour until they are completely soft and golden—they must not brown. Stir in the chopped rosemary.

Preheat the oven to 450°F. Punch down the dough with your hands and roll out, or stretch with your fingers, to a rectangle or 12-inch circle on the baking sheet. Spoon the onions on top of the pizza and spread them evenly. Dot with the mozzarella, anchovies, and olives. Sprinkle with olive oil.

Bake in the preheated oven for 15–20 minutes until golden and crisp. Top with rosemary leaves and serve immediately.

fish and seafood

spaghetti and shrimp with pesto, cooked in a paper package

spaghetti con gamberi al cartoccio

This is a deliciously novel way of cooking pasta—it seals in all the juices and releases a wonderful aroma when the package is opened.

Cook the spaghetti in plenty of boiling salted water for 2 minutes only, then drain and mix with half the pesto.

Cut 4 pieces of waxed paper, 12 inches square, and brush 1 teaspoon olive oil over the center of each. Pile equal amounts of pasta in the middle of each square. Put the remaining pesto in a bowl, add the garlic and shrimp, and toss well. Divide between the squares. Season with black pepper and sprinkle each serving with 2 tablespoons wine.

Brush the edges of each paper square lightly with water, then bring up the paper loosely around the filling, twisting tightly to seal. (The packages should look like gathered money bags). Put the packages on the baking sheet.

Bake in a preheated oven at 400°F for 10–15 minutes. Serve immediately, letting guests open their own packages.

16 oz. spaghetti or similar pasta

⅔ cup store-bought or homemade pesto sauce

olive oil, for brushing

1 garlic clove, crushed

1½ lb. medium uncooked shrimp tails, shells on

freshly ground black pepper

¼ cup dry white wine

waxed paper

a baking sheet

serves 4

oven-baked tuna with salsa

tonno al forno con salmoriglio

Fresh tuna bakes very well in the oven, especially if marinated first to keep it moist. I have taken the liberty of adding capers and mint to the traditional salmoriglio *sauce adored by Sicilians. The capers add a sharp edge to the sauce, and cut through the richness of the fish.*

Put the olive oil, garlic, oregano, wine, salt, and pepper in a bowl and stir well. Spread half the lemon slices in the ovenproof dish and put the tuna steaks on top. Pour over the olive oil mixture and put the remaining lemon slices on top. Set aside for 30 minutes.

Meanwhile, to make the salsa, soak the capers in water for 10 minutes, drain, pat dry, and chop if large. Put the vinegar and sugar in a bowl and stir until dissolved. Add the lemon zest and juice. Beat in the olive oil, then add the garlic, chopped mint, and capers. Set aside to infuse.

Bake the tuna in a preheated oven at 350°F for about 12 minutes. The fish should be just cooked in the center—it can be served slightly pink. Lift onto warm plates, leaving the juices behind. Serve with the salsa spooned on top.

3 tablespoons good olive oil

4 garlic cloves, crushed

1 teaspoon dried oregano

¼ cup dry white wine

1 lemon, thinly sliced

4 thick tuna steaks, 6–8 oz. each

sea salt and freshly ground black pepper

caper and mint salsa

1 tablespoon salted capers, drained

2 tablespoons red wine vinegar

1–2 teaspoons sugar

finely grated zest and juice of ½ unwaxed lemon

¼ cup good olive oil

1 garlic clove, finely chopped

2 tablespoons finely chopped fresh mint

a non-aluminum ovenproof dish

serves 4

The rose and gold skin of the red snapper looks beautiful with the deep red of the blood oranges. If you can't find blood oranges, use regular oranges instead. Citrus fruits are often cooked with fish in Italy—their gentle acidity brings out the sweetness of the flesh. I like these cooked without wine, but you could add a tablespoon to each package if tempted. The beautiful aroma when you open them is wonderful.

red snapper and blood oranges cooked in a package
triglie e *tarocchi al cartoccio*

Cut 4 rectangles of parchment paper or aluminum foil large enough to wrap each fish loosely. Brush with a little oil.

Grate the zest from the oranges into a bowl, then mix in the olive oil, salt, and pepper and set aside. Peel the oranges as you would an apple, removing all the white pith, then slice the flesh thinly. Put 1 bay leaf in the cavity of each fish and 1 on top. Put a pile of orange slices on one side of each parchment square, using half the orange slices in total. Put the fish on the oranges and cover them with the remaining orange slices. Sprinkle with the oil and orange zest mixture, then add the olives. Season well.

If you have a water sprayer, spritz the inside of the paper lightly. Fold the paper loosely over the fish and twist the edges together. Lift onto the baking sheet. Bake in a preheated oven at 375°F for 20 minutes.

Serve on warm plates, letting guests open their own packages.

4 small red snapper, 8 oz. each, carefully scaled, cleaned, and filleted

2 tablespoons extra virgin olive oil, plus extra for brushing

2 oranges, preferably tarocchi or blood oranges

8 fresh bay leaves

20 small black olives, such as Niçoise

sea salt and freshly ground black pepper

parchment paper or foil

a baking sheet

serves 4

braised sea bass with fennel and green olives

brazino al forno con finocchio

This is the perfect way to cook a whole, firm-fleshed fish. It will keep the flesh moist, while the skin protects it. Fennel and olives are also distinctive Mediterranean flavors.

Wash the fish inside and out and fill the cavity with sprigs of rosemary.

Cut the fennel bulbs in half lengthwise, cut out the cores, then slice thickly. Blanch in a large saucepan of salted boiling water for 5 minutes, then drain.

Put the oil, lemon juice, herbs, salt, and pepper in a medium bowl, beat well, then stir in the fennel to coat. Transfer to the ovenproof dish. Put the fish on top of the fennel and spoon over any remaining liquid. Tuck in the olives and pour the wine over the top.

Bake in a preheated oven at 425°F for 30 minutes. Open the oven and baste with the juices and stir the fennel around. Turn off the oven and leave for 5 minutes for the fish to "set." Serve immediately.

2½ lb. sea bass, grouper, or rockfish, scaled and cleaned

a few sprigs of rosemary

2 large fennel bulbs

⅔ cup good olive oil

freshly squeezed juice of 1 lemon

1 tablespoon dried oregano

3 tablespoons chopped fresh flat-leaf parsley

8 large green olives, pitted

⅔ cup dry white wine

sea salt and freshly ground black pepper

a shallow ovenproof dish

serves 4

fish baked in a salt crust

pesce alla crosta di sale

This excellent method of cooking fish conserves the juices without in any way oversalting the flesh. The salt bakes hard to form a protective crust so that the fish cooks in its own juices—the skin protects it from the salt. It's a nice idea to stuff the cavity with fresh herbs and sliced lemon before burying the fish in salt.

at least 2 lb. kosher salt

1 egg white

2–4 lb. whole large firm-fleshed fish, cleaned but not scaled

a tomato salad, to serve

a long ovenproof dish (choose one that will comfortably hold the whole fish)

serves 4–6

Pour enough salt into the dish to make a layer 1 inch thick. Mix the egg white with 3 tablespoons water and sprinkle half the liquid over the salt. Set the fish on the salt bed and pour enough salt around and over it to cover it completely. Sprinkle with the remaining egg white and water.

Bake the fish in a preheated oven at 375°F for 45 minutes to 1 hour.

Remove from the oven and put the dish, with the fish still encased in its snowy armor, in the middle of the table.

Crack open the salt crust with a rolling pin. Remove the shards of salt crust and peel back the skin to reveal perfectly cooked, succulent flesh without a trace of saltiness. Serve with a simple tomato salad.

When opened up and boned, sardines cook in minutes in a hot oven. Marinating them in oil and lemon juice lends piquancy to the delicate flesh. This is a good dish to prepare a day ahead, then serve for lunch with salad.

sardines baked with garlic, lemon, olive oil, and bread crumbs

sarde al gratin

Scale the sardines with the blunt edge of a knife. Cut off the heads and slit open the bellies. Remove the guts under running water. Slide your thumb along the backbone to release the flesh along its length. Take hold of the backbone at the head end and lift it out. The fish should now be open flat like a book.

Put the oil, lemon zest, and juice in a large bowl, beat well, then stir in the garlic, parsley, capers, salt, and pepper. Holding each sardine by the tail, dip in the lemony olive oil, then put skin side up in the ovenproof dish. Pour in any remaining liquid, sprinkle with the bread crumbs, and bake in a preheated oven at 400°F for 15 minutes.

Serve warm immediately, or let cool, then store overnight in the refrigerator. Serve the next day at room temperature, when the sardines will have marinated in the oil, lemon, and herbs. Add the parsley and lemon wedges, then serve.

8 fresh whole sardines

⅓ cup good olive oil

finely grated zest and juice of 1 unwaxed lemon

2 garlic cloves, thinly sliced

3 tablespoons chopped fresh flat-leaf parsley

1 tablespoon salted capers, drained and chopped

3 tablespoons dried bread crumbs

sea salt and freshly ground black pepper

to serve

extra chopped parley

lemon wedges

a shallow ovenproof dish

serves 4

meat and poultry

A memorable way of roasting a chicken—all the flavors permeate the flesh during its time in the oven, and the smell in the kitchen is wonderful. This dish is particularly good cold, eaten at a picnic.

chicken roasted with bay leaves, lemon, and garlic

pollo arrosto con alloro, limone e aglio

1 free-range chicken about 3 lb.

1 lemon, very thinly sliced

3 garlic cloves, thinly sliced

6 small fresh bay leaves (or use sage or even basil), plus extra bay leaves to make a bed

a little olive oil

sea salt and freshly ground black pepper

a roasting pan

serves 6

Starting at the vent end of the chicken, slide your hand carefully underneath the skin of each breast to loosen it. Push 3–4 slices of lemon under the skin of each breast, slide the garlic slices on top, then finish with 3 bay leaves on each side. Smooth down the skin. Rub with olive oil, then salt and pepper.

Arrange a bed of bay leaves in the roasting pan and put the remaining lemon slices on top. Put the chicken on top and roast in a preheated oven at 375°F for 20 minutes per pound, plus 20 minutes extra, basting every now and then, until golden brown, crisp, and cooked through. To check, push a skewer into the thickest part of the thigh—the juices should run clear and golden. If there is any trace of pink, cook for 5–10 minutes longer.

Serve hot, or cool, chill, and serve cold.

polenta baked with italian sausage and cheese

pasticcio di polenta con salsicce e taleggio

2 cups yellow cornmeal, preferably stoneground, or quick-cook polenta

1 lb. fresh Italian sausages

1 tablespoon olive oil

1 red onion, finely chopped

⅔ cup vegetable or meat stock

3 tablespoons chopped fresh rosemary and sage, mixed

12 oz. Taleggio cheese, chopped or grated, 3½ cups

1½ cups freshly grated Parmesan cheese

a few pieces of butter

sea salt and freshly ground black pepper

a shallow ovenproof dish, buttered

serves 6

Bring 5 cups water to a boil in a larger saucepan. Gradually whisk in the cornmeal and 1 teaspoon salt. Reduce the heat to low, and cook, stirring constantly with a wooden spoon, until the cornmeal is very thick. Transfer from the pan to a wooden board and shape into a mound. Let cool and set. If using quick-cook polenta, cook according to the package instructions.

Slice the sausages very thickly. Heat the olive oil in a nonstick skillet, add the sausage, and sauté until browned on all sides. Add the onion and cook for 5 minutes until softening. Add the stock and half the chopped herbs, salt, and pepper.

Cut the polenta into ½-inch slices. Arrange a layer of polenta in the prepared dish. Add half the sausage mixture, half the Taleggio, and half the Parmesan, in layers. Cover with another layer of polenta, add layers of the remaining sausage mixture, Taleggio, and Parmesan, and dot with a few pieces of butter. Sprinkle with the remaining herbs.

Bake in a preheated oven at 350°F for 40 minutes until brown and bubbling.

A real winter warmer to eat by a roaring fire. This is sublime comfort food, loaded with sausage and strings of melting cheese. At the risk of being sacrilegious, Spanish chorizo would be great in this dish. Add chopped herbs to the polenta or even a little chopped chile.

This classic Tuscan dish deserves its place in any book entitled Al Forno. Redolent of the early morning markets where porchetta *is sold crammed into huge buns, this dish re-creates all those tastes and smells in your oven at home. Use plenty of rosemary so that the sweet pork flesh will be suffused with its pungent aroma. Tuscans cook the pork on the bone, then slice it into thick chops—I think this is a more elegant way to cook it.*

pork loin roasted with rosemary and garlic

arista alla fiorentina

1 boneless center-cut pork loin roast (about 3 lb.)

6 large garlic cloves

¼ cup chopped fresh rosemary

1¼ cups dry white wine

sprigs of fresh rosemary

olive oil, for brushing

sea salt and freshly ground black pepper

2 roasting tins

serves 6

Turn the loin fat side down. Make deep slits all over, especially in the thick part. Put the garlic, rosemary, and at least a teaspoon of salt and pepper (more will give a truly authentic Tuscan flavor) into a food processor and blend to a paste. Push this paste into all the slits in the meat and spread the remainder over the surface of the meat. Roll up and tie with fine twine.

Weigh the meat and calculate the cooking time, allowing 25 minutes for every 1 lb. At this stage you can cover with plastic wrap and chill for several hours to deepen the flavor. When ready to cook, preheat the oven to 450°F, or a high as your oven will go. Uncover the pork and brown all over in a hot skillet. Set in the roasting pan. Pour the wine over the pork and tuck in the rosemary sprigs.

Roast for 20 minutes. Turn down the heat to 400°F, and roast for the remaining calculated time, basting the pork loin every 20 minutes.

Rest the pork in a warm place for 15 minutes before carving into thick slices. Serve with the pan juices.

leg of lamb "seven hills of rome"

coscia di agnello "sette colli di Roma"

This leg of lamb is braised until cooked and tender, then roasted to color it. The powerful flavorings melt into the meat, with the anchovies disappearing to leave a lingering salty note. This way of cooking lamb stems from the days of the Roman Empire, when the most popular condiment was a sauce made from fermented fish.

3 lb. leg of lamb

2 tablespoons olive oil

10 juniper berries

3 garlic cloves, crushed

2 oz. canned anchovies

1 tablespoon chopped fresh rosemary

2 tablespoons balsamic vinegar

2 sprigs of rosemary

2 fresh bay leaves

1¼ cups dry white wine

sprigs of fresh thyme

sea salt and freshly ground black pepper

a flameproof casserole dish (into which the lamb should fit snugly)

serves 6

Trim the lamb of any excess fat. Heat the oil in the casserole dish, add the lamb, and brown it all over. Remove and cool quickly.

Crush 6 of the juniper berries, the garlic, anchovies, and chopped rosemary with a mortar and pestle. Stir in the vinegar and mix to a paste. Using a small, sharp knife, make many small incisions into the lamb. Spread the paste all over the meat, working it into the incisions, then season with salt and pepper.

Put the rosemary sprigs and bay leaves in the casserole dish and set the lamb on top. Pour in the wine. Crush the remaining juniper berries and add to the lamb, then add the thyme. Cover, bring to a boil on top of the stove, then braise in a preheated oven at 325°F for 1 hour, turning the lamb every 20 minutes.

Raise the oven temperature to 400°F. Roast uncovered for another 45 minutes or until browned—the lamb should be very tender and cooked through.

Transfer the lamb to a serving dish and keep it warm. Skim off the fat from the pan, then boil the sauce, adding a little water if necessary and scraping up the sediment. Season with salt and pepper if necessary and serve with the lamb.

Cut the meat into very large chunks—long, slow cooking tenderizes it perfectly. Served with boiled potatoes and green vegetables, it's a good dish for a crowd.

beef braised in red wine

brasato al barolo

Pour the wine into a large saucepan and bring to a boil. Boil hard until reduced by half (leaving 3 cups). Let cool completely.

Cut the meat into 2-inch pieces. Put in a large plastic bag with the onions, carrots, celery, bay leaves, thyme, peppercorns, and allspice. Pour in the cooled wine. Shake the bag to mix, then seal the bag and put it in a large bowl to marinate in the refrigerator overnight.

Open the bag and pour the contents into a colander set over a bowl. Separate the meat from the vegetable mixture and pat the pieces dry with paper towels. Reserve the wine.

Heat the oil in the casserole dish on top of the stove and brown the meat well in batches. Return the meat to the dish, then stir in the vegetable mixture. Add the reserved wine and stir in the tomato paste. Add enough stock to cover the meat and vegetables. Bring to a boil, reduce the heat, cover, and cook in a preheated oven at 325°F for 2–3 hours until very tender. Top up the liquid with extra stock if it evaporates too quickly. Alternatively, the dish may be simmered gently on top of the stove for 2–3 hours.

Using a slotted spoon, transfer the meat to a bowl. Discard the bay leaves. Pour the sauce into a blender or food processor and blend until smooth (the sauce will look pale, but will darken when reheated). Add salt and pepper to taste. The sauce should be quite thick—if not, boil to reduce it. Stir the meat back into the sauce, reheat, sprinkle with parsley, and serve.

2 bottles Barolo or other good-quality red wine, 750 ml each

3 lb. boneless stewing beef, such as chuck, or bottom round, well trimmed

2 onions, coarsely chopped

2 carrots, chopped

1 celery stalk, chopped

2 bay leaves

2 large sprigs of thyme

6 peppercorns

2 allspice berries, crushed

3 tablespoons olive oil

2 tablespoons tomato paste

about 1½ quarts beef stock, to cover

sea salt and freshly ground black pepper

chopped fresh flat-leaf parsley, to serve

a large flameproof casserole dish

serves 6–8

rolled beef simmered in tomato sauce

polpettone al forno

A traditional recipe from the Naples area, in which a lean piece of beef is rolled around a savory stuffing and slowly cooked in a tomato and vegetable sauce. The sauce is usually served tossed with pasta as an appetizer, the meat served as the entrée with just a little sauce, followed by a salad or a plate of green vegetables.

Soak the bread crumbs in a little water. Soak the currants in lukewarm water for 15 minutes, then drain. Put the beef between 2 sheets of plastic wrap and beat out with a meat mallet or rolling pin to flatten slightly to about ¼ inch thick. Season with salt and pepper.

Lightly squeeze out the soaked bread crumbs and put in a bowl. Add two-thirds of the chopped prosciutto, the parsley, garlic, marjoram, and egg yolks, season with salt and pepper, and mix well. Spread this mixture over the beef and sprinkle with the drained currants and the pine nuts. Roll up the beef, tucking in the sides, and tie up with kitchen twine.

Heat the oil in the casserole dish on top of the stove, add the rolled beef, and brown it all over. Transfer to a plate. Add the remaining prosciutto, the clove, onion, carrot, and celery to the dish and cook for 10 minutes until the vegetables are soft. Stir in the tomato paste and 1 cup warm water.

Return the rolled beef to the dish and bring to a boil. Cover with the circle of waxed paper and a lid, then transfer to a preheated oven at 350°F for about 2 hours, adding a little extra water every now and then. When cooked, lift the beef out onto a warm plate, cover, and set aside.

Pour the contents of the dish into a blender and work to a purée. Reheat and taste for seasoning. To serve, slice the beef thickly and serve with a little sauce ladled over. Pass the remaining sauce separately, or use for pasta.

2½ cups fresh bread crumbs

1 tablespoon currants

1 slice of lean rump or bottom round steak, 1 lb., cut ½ inch thick

6 oz. prosciutto, finely chopped

⅓ cup chopped fresh flat-leaf parsley

1 garlic clove, finely chopped

½ teaspoon dried marjoram

2 egg yolks

1 tablespoon pine nuts

2 tablespoons olive oil

1 whole clove

1 small onion, finely chopped

1 small carrot, finely chopped

1 celery stalk, finely chopped

2 tablespoons tomato paste

sea salt and freshly ground black pepper

a large flameproof casserole dish

a circle of waxed paper

serves 4

sweet things

This is one of the best ways of cooking pears I know. It is so simple to make, but tastes very luxurious. Choose pears that are ripe but not too soft, or they will overcook in the oven. If you can't get a good rich Marsala or Vin Santo, use sweet sherry or Madeira instead.

caramelized pears with marsala and mascarpone cream

pere al forno con marsala e mascarpone

Cut the pears in half and scoop out the cores—do not peel them. Sprinkle the sugar into the pan or dish. Set over medium heat and let the sugar melt and caramelize. Remove from the heat as soon as it reaches a medium-brown color and quickly arrange the pears cut side down in the caramel.

Bake in a preheated oven at 375°F until the pears are soft, 20–25 minutes. Carefully lift out the pears and transfer to an ovenproof serving dish, keeping the caramel in the pan.

Put the pan on top of the stove over medium heat and add the Marsala or Vin Santo. Bring to a boil, stirring to dislodge any set caramel, and boil fast until reduced and syrupy. Set aside.

Scoop out a good teaspoon from each cooked pear and put it in a bowl. Add the mascarpone and vanilla seeds and beat well. Fill the centers of the pears with the mascarpone mixture. Return to the oven for 5 minutes until the mascarpone has heated through. Serve with the caramel sauce spooned over the top.

6 large ripe pears

¼ cup sugar

⅔ cup Marsala wine or Vin Santo

8 oz. mascarpone cheese

1 vanilla bean, split, seeds scraped out and reserved

a flameproof, ovenproof pan or dish

serves 6

figs baked with vanilla and lemon

fichi al forno con vaniglia e limone

Ripe figs need almost nothing done to them—but if you bake them with lots of vanilla and lemon-scented sugar, and hide a walnut in the middle of each one, you will end up with something divine. Take care not to overcook them or they will collapse.

12 large ripe figs
12 walnuts halves
2 plump vanilla beans
⅔ cup sugar
**grated zest of
1 unwaxed lemon**
**3 tablespoons
white wine**
**heavy cream or
ice cream, to serve**

a shallow ovenproof dish

serves 6

Cut a deep cross in the top of each fig so that they open up a little. Push a walnut half into each cross. Pack the figs closely together in the baking dish.

Chop the vanilla beans and put into a food processor. Add the sugar and lemon zest and process until the beans and lemon zest are chopped into tiny bits. Spoon the mixture over each fig and around the dish. Moisten with white wine.

Bake in a preheated oven at 450°F for 10 minutes until the sugar melts and the figs start to caramelize. Remove from the oven and let cool for a few minutes before serving with cream. Alternatively, serve cold with ice cream.

These cookies are deliciously buttery and crunchy, and fantastic dipped into Vin Santo or caffellatte. The word biscotti, *when used as an adjective, means "twice-cooked"—these are cooked once in a log, then sliced and cooked again to dry them out. I like to add cornmeal for a slightly gritty texture.*

hazelnut and chocolate biscotti
biscotti alle nocciole e cioccolato

Spread the hazelnuts on a baking sheet and toast in a preheated oven at 325°F for 5–10 minutes until they begin to release their aromas. Transfer the hazelnuts to a clean dish towel and rub off the skins. Let cool. Leave the oven on.

Put the butter and sugar in a bowl and beat until pale and creamy. Beat in the egg, vanilla extract, and rum. Using a separate bowl, sift together the flour, cocoa, baking powder, and salt, then stir in the cornmeal. Fold into the butter and egg mixture. Stir in the toasted hazelnuts.

Transfer the dough to a floured work surface and knead until smooth. The dough should be soft but not sticky—if it feels sticky, add a little more flour. Divide the dough into 4 pieces. Roll into logs about 2 inches wide and ½ inch deep. Flatten them slightly, then put on the prepared baking sheets. Bake for 35 minutes or until just golden around the edges.

Let cool slightly then, using a serrated knife, cut diagonally into ½-inch slices. Arrange cut side down on the baking sheets and bake for another 10–15 minutes until golden brown and crisp. (Take care not to let them burn, or they will taste bitter.) Transfer to a wire rack to cool. Store in an airtight container for up to 1 week.

1⅓ cups whole hazelnuts

1 stick plus 2 tablespoons unsalted butter, softened

1 cup sugar

2 eggs, beaten

2 teaspoon vanilla extract

1 tablespoon dark rum

2 cups all-purpose flour

¾ cup unsweetened cocoa powder

1½ teaspoons baking powder

½ teaspoon salt

½ cup coarse cornmeal

2 baking sheets, lined with parchment paper

a wire rack

makes about 30

grandmother's cake
torta della nonna

Everyone in Italy knows this fabulous tart filled with pastry cream and topped with pine nuts. All baking grandmothers have their own version. There is a chocolate version called torta del nonno—grandfather's cake. *Instead of the ¼ cup flour, use 1 tablespoon flour and 3 tablespoons cocoa powder when you make the custard.*

Put the butter and sugar in a bowl and beat until pale and creamy. Beat in the egg yolks, orange zest, vanilla extract, and salt. Work in the flour until almost mixed. Transfer to a work surface and knead gently until smooth. Cut into 2 pieces—one slightly bigger than the other. Form into disks, wrap in plastic, and chill for at least 30 minutes. Roll out the larger half as thinly as possible and use to line the tart pan.

Prick the base of the tart and put in the freezer for at least 15 minutes. Line the tart with foil or waxed paper, fill with baking beans, and bake in a preheated oven at 375°F for 15 minutes. Remove the beans and paper or foil and return to the oven for 10 minutes to dry out. Remove from the oven and let cool. Leave the oven on.

Meanwhile heat the milk until just about to boil, then take off the heat. Beat the egg yolks and sugar in a bowl, then beat in the flour. Pour the milk onto the flour mixture, then whisk well. Return to the pan and heat gently, stirring until thickening. When it reaches a very slow boil, let boil for 2 minutes, then stir in the vanilla extract. Pour into the cooled pie crust. Let cool.

When cold, roll out the remaining dough to a circle slightly larger than the diameter of the pan. Brush the edges of the crust with some of beaten egg yolk and cover with the dough circle, pressing it firmly onto the cooked edges and trimming the excess. Brush the dough with more egg yolk and sprinkle with pine nuts. Using a skewer, make a couple of air holes in the top. Bake for 1 hour, then remove and let cool completely. Dust with confectioners' sugar and serve.

1½ sticks unsalted butter, softened

1 cup confectioners' sugar

2 egg yolks

finely grated zest of 1 unwaxed orange

1 teaspoon vanilla extract

a pinch of salt

1⅔ cups all-purpose flour

custard filling

2¾ cups milk

2 egg yolks

⅓ cup sugar

¼ cup all-purpose flour or cornstarch

½ teaspoon vanilla extract

to finish

1 beaten egg yolk

¼ cup pine nuts

confectioners' sugar

a tart pan with removable base, 9 inches diameter

foil or waxed paper and baking beans or weights

makes one 9-inch tart, to serve 8

index

B
beans simmered in a Chianti flask, 19
beef:
    braised in red wine, 52
    rolled beef simmered in tomato
        sauce, 55
biscotti: hazelnut and chocolate
    biscotti, 61

C
cake: grandmother's cake, 62
chicken roasted with bay leaves,
    lemon, and garlic, 45

E
eggplant, tomato, and Parmesan
    gratin, 14

F
figs baked with vanilla and lemon, 58
fish:
    braised bass with fennel and
        green olives, 39
    fish baked in a salt crust, 40
    red snapper and red oranges
        cooked in a package, 37
    sardines baked with garlic,
        lemon, olive oil, and bread
        crumbs, 43
    tuna: oven-baked tuna with
        salsa, 34

L
lamb "seven hills of Rome," 50

O
onions:
    and rosemary schiacciata, 31
    whole onions baked in their
        skins, 10

P
pasta: cannelloni with ricotta, bitter
    greens, and cherry tomato
    sauce, 28

fresh egg pasta and fresh
    spinach pasta, 24
green lasagne with ricotta,
    pesto, and mushrooms, 27
spaghetti and shrimp with pesto,
    cooked in a bag, 33
pears: caramelized pears with
    Marsala wine and
    mascarpone cream, 57
pizza: onion, mozzarella, and
    rosemary schiacciata, 31
polenta baked with Italian sausage
    and cheese, 46
pork loin roasted with rosemary
    and garlic, 49
potato and mushroom gratin, 17
shrimp: spaghetti and shrimp
    with pesto, cooked in a
    bag, 33

R
rice: three-colored rice and cheese
    cake, 23

T
tomatoes:
    cannelloni with ricotta, bitter
        greens, and cherry tomato
        sauce, 28
    eggplant, tomato, and Parmesan
        gratin, 14
    meat roll simmered in tomato
        sauce, 55
    slow-roasted tomatoes with
        garlic and oregano, 9
    spinach and ricotta timbales with
        sun-dried tomatoes, olives,
        capers, and herbs, 20
    zucchini and tomatoes baked
        with fontina, 13

Z
zucchini and tomatoes baked with
    fontina, 13

conversion charts

Weights and measures have been rounded up or down slightly to make measuring easier.

Volume equivalents:

American	Metric	Imperial
1 teaspoon	5 ml	
1 tablespoon	15 ml	
¼ cup	60 ml	2 fl.oz.
⅓ cup	75 ml	2½ fl.oz.
½ cup	125 ml	4 fl.oz.
⅔ cup	150 ml	5 fl.oz. (¼ pint)
¾ cup	175 ml	6 fl.oz.
1 cup	250 ml	8 fl.oz.

Weight equivalents: Measurements:

Imperial	Metric	Inches	Cm
1 oz.	25 g	¼ inch	5 mm
2 oz.	50 g	½ inch	1 cm
3 oz.	75 g	¾ inch	1.5 cm
4 oz.	125 g	1 inch	2.5 cm
5 oz.	150 g	2 inches	5 cm
6 oz.	175 g	3 inches	7 cm
7 oz.	200 g	4 inches	10 cm
8 oz. (½ lb.)	250 g	5 inches	12 cm
9 oz.	275 g	6 inches	15 cm
10 oz.	300 g	7 inches	18 cm
11 oz.	325 g	8 inches	20 cm
12 oz.	375 g	9 inches	23 cm
13 oz.	400 g	10 inches	25 cm
14 oz.	425 g	11 inches	28 cm
15 oz.	475 g	12 inches	30 cm
16 oz. (1 lb.)	500 g		
2 1b.	1 kg		

Oven temperatures:

110°C	(225°F)	Gas ¼
120°C	(250°F)	Gas ½
140°C	(275°F)	Gas 1
150°C	(300°F)	Gas 2
160°C	(325°F)	Gas 3
180°C	(350°F)	Gas 4
190°C	(375°F)	Gas 5
200°C	(400°F)	Gas 6
220°C	(425°F)	Gas 7
230°C	(450°F)	Gas 8
240°C	(475°F)	Gas 9